Published in Great Britain in MMXXII by
The Salariya Book Company Ltd
25 Marlborough Place, Brighton BN1 1UB
www.salariya.com

ISBN: 978-1-913971-43-4

© The Salariya Book Company Ltd MMXXII
All rights reserved. No part of this publication may be reproduced, stored in or introduced into a retrieval system or transmitted in any form, or by any means (electronic, mechanical, photocopying, recording or otherwise) without the written permission of the publisher. Any person who does any unauthorised act in relation to this publication may be liable to criminal prosecution and civil claims for damages.

1 3 5 7 9 8 6 4 2

A CIP catalogue record for this book is available from the British Library.
Printed and bound in Malta.

This book is sold subject to the conditions that it shall not, by way of trade or otherwise, be lent, resold, hired out, or otherwise circulated without the publisher's prior consent in any form or binding or cover other than that in which it is published and without similar condition being imposed on the subsequent purchaser.

Author: John Townsend
Illustrator: Rory Walker
Editor: Nick Pierce

Visit
www.salariya.com
for our online catalogue and
free fun stuff.

The TV crew and television show in this book are works of fiction. Names, characters, businesses, places, events, locales and incidents are either the products of the author's imagination or used in a fictitious manner. Any resemblance to actual persons, TV crews or television shows in the present or the past, or actual events, is purely coincidental. The ghosts are all real!

LIVE FROM THE CRYPT

Interviews with the Ghosts of Roman Emperors

Series created by
David Salariya

Written by
John Townsend

Illustrated by
Rory Walker

SALARIYA
Brilliant Books Make Brilliant Children

Meet the cast

TV crew:

Mish Varma: Host of Live from the Crypt TV show
Jonty Yardley: Co-host of Live from the Crypt TV show
Larna Obata: Reporter
Mandy: Hair & Make-up
Binti: Director
Kev: Camera operator
Aleema: Newsreader/general presenter
Duncan: Special Correspondent
Gail Forse: Forecast presenter
Professor Barbitium: Roman historian

Ghost Guests:

Emperor Augustus (63 BC–AD 14): Reign (27 BC–AD 14)
Empress Livia (Julia Augusta) (58/59 BC–AD 29): (Wife of Augustus)
Emperor Tiberius (42 BC–AD 37): Reign (AD 14–AD 37)
Empress Julia the Elder (39 BC–AD 14): (Wife of Tiberius)
Emperor Caligula (AD 12–41): Reign (AD 37–41)
Empress Milonia Caesonia (AD ?–41): (Wife of Caligula)
Emperor Claudius (10 BC–AD 54): Reign (AD 41–54)
Empress Agrippina the Younger (AD 15–59): (Wife of Claudius)
Emperor Nero (AD 37–68): Reign (AD 54–68)
Empress Claudia Octavia (AD 40–62): (Wife of Nero)

Interviews with the Ghosts of Roman Emperors

Contents

Introduction	7
Welcome to the programme	11
No script from the crypt	21
Comic strip 1: How it all began	28
Behind the scenes	33
Commercial break	44
In a nutshell	55
Comic strip 2: Emperor Augustus	62
Spot the emperor	67
Comic strip 3: Tiberius	76
Spin the news	81
Comic strip 4: Caligula	86
How nice to meet you	91
Comic strip 5: Claudius	100
Forecast	105
Comic strip 6: Boudicca fights back	108
Ghosts reunited	113
Comic strip 7: Agrippina ('The Younger') strikes	122
I'm a Cel-emperor... Get Me Out of Here!	127
Comic strip 8: Nero	142
Who am I?	147
Roman emperors' family tree	158
Timeline	160
Quiz – Decies centena millia, qui vult vincere? (Who wants to win a million?)	164
Glossary	169
Live from the Crypt – In the classroom	170
Index	176

Interviews with the Ghosts of Roman Emperors

Introduction

Just imagine it... the TV crew arrives on location in Italy at the Mausoleum of Augustus in Rome, beside the River Tiber.

Here are the remains of an ancient tomb, originally built in 28 BC by Roman Emperor Augustus. This grand round monument, the largest circular crypt in the world, is a famous burial chamber containing urns full of ashes — the remains of ancient Rome's most famous families.

The first Roman Emperor and his wife are among those hidden inside. Tonight the cameras are waiting for their ghosts to stir. Never interviewed before on live TV, they may be ready to speak at last...
How can ghosts surrounded by scandal and gossip refuse the invitation to talk on camera and put the record straight?
What if the TV floor-manager, tea boy, technicians, make-up team, reporters, presenters and director are all waiting nervously for a 'live encounter with the dead'?

What if we switch on at home for the TV show they said could never be done: *Live from the Crypt*?

Sit back and dare to be stunned...

Stand-by for lights, cameras, music —

ACTION...

Interviews with the Ghosts of Roman Emperors

Interviews with the Ghosts of Roman Emperors

Welcome to the programme

MISH:

Hello and welcome to another of our crypt programmes coming to you live...

JONTY:

With a few dead ingredients – in our new series *Live from the Crypt.*

MISH:

With Jonty Yardley and me, Mish Varma.

JONTY:

Your ghost-hunters searching for some of the most famous ghosts in history.

MISH:

And tonight, we've come to Rome to meet the first five emperors of the Roman Empire and some of their families – we hope.

JONTY:

Yes, we're at The Mausoleum of Augustus... sitting in the spooky moonlight for an outside broadcast like nothing seen before.

MISH:

Inside the creepy crypt behind us are the remains of some of the most famous Romans from around two thousand years ago – and rumours say their ghosts linger around here, too.

JONTY:

So we're hoping to meet them LIVE and invite them out for a chat on our sofa.

MISH:

Yes, our set tonight is inside a small gazebo with a tasteful mosaic floor to make our guests feel at home, along with marble statues and ancient Roman pottery.

Interviews with the Ghosts of Roman Emperors

JONTY:
While I am dressed in a toga and sandals...

MISH:
Caligae?

JONTY:
No, from eBay.

MISH:
Caligae are footwear. I hope you've got your subligaculum firmly fastened, Jonty.

JONTY:
I have no idea what you mean.

MISH:
Underwear. A subligaculum was worn by men and women, especially by Roman gladiators, athletes and actors. I suppose you could say it was Latin for classy knickers.

JONTY:
Probably too much information. Anyway, I'm very excited – and terrified – at the prospect of meeting

the ghosts of the first emperors and empresses of Rome. Some of them were brutal tyrants, you know.

MISH:

I guess they were certainly extremely colourful characters. If any of them turn nasty on our show, the director will have to cut to a commercial break.

JONTY:

Cutting out a couple of emperors might need a sharp pair of Caesars. Did you see what I did there?

MISH:

This is a serious show, Jonty. Moving on... as the mausoleum is dedicated to the first ever emperor, we're hoping to meet him and his wife.

JONTY:

Yes, Emperor Augustus and his third wife, Empress Livia, will hopefully be our first Roman guests on *Live from the Crypt*. The month of August was named after him, you know.

Interviews with the Ghosts of Roman Emperors

MISH:

That's right, even though he was also known as Octavian.

JONTY:

Maybe they called October after him, too.

MISH:

No, Jonty – you haven't done your homework. October got its name from the Latin 'octo', meaning 'eight', as it used to be the eighth month.

JONTY:

Well, I expect March got its name from all the Roman soldiers on the march every spring.

MISH:

No, Jonty. The Romans named March after Mars, the Roman god of war.

JONTY:

Fair enough. Actually, I have done research as I know Augustus came to power after the assassination of Julius Caesar in 44 BC. Then, after seventeen years, he became the first actual Emperor

of Rome, the title he held for over forty years. Today he's remembered as one of the great leaders in European history.

MISH:

Yes, and one of the better emperors. He grew the Roman empire, was popular and lived to a ripe old age without getting assassinated, like many other Roman rulers. Then his stepson took over – a different kind of leader, entirely.

JONTY:

Ah yes, Tiberius. His mother was Augustus' third wife – the beautiful yet scheming Livia Drusilla. She's also in the mausoleum, so we're hoping to meet her ghost as well. She was quite a scary empress, by all accounts.

MISH:

Then you'd better be careful, Jonty. None of your bad jokes. Livia was a devoted wife and could be quite ruthless to protect her husband and son.

JONTY:

I'll do my best to impress the empress with success – no stress, I guess.

Interviews with the Ghosts of Roman Emperors

MISH:

Moving on... our on-the-spot reporter is about to enter the crypt to find those ancient dusty urns containing the ashes of the early Caesars. Rome is said to be haunted by many ghosts from ancient times.

JONTY:

Then let's go live to Larna, who is creeping about inside the mausoleum hoping to meet some of the famous ghostly inhabitants.

MISH:

Yes, Jonty, our special night-cameras are set up as midnight approaches – the time when ghosts are meant to stir and walk around.

JONTY:

I can't wait to hear them talk, even though my ancient Italian is a bit rusty.

MISH:

No worries – a special app is fitted to our equipment to translate Latin into English.

JONTY:

Praeclarus! That means 'excellent', by the way.

MISH:

And vivet in crypta is 'live from the crypt'. I think.

JONTY:

I can already hear in my earpiece that Larna is sensing a presence in the tomb.

MISH:

Then we'll stop talking and let Larna see what develops, totally unscripted.

JONTY:

(whispering) So we now join Larna LIVE for 'No script at the crypt'. We're gripped!

Interviews with the Ghosts of Roman Emperors

No Script from the crypt

LARNA:
> *(whispering)* I'm shining a torch onto a row of ancient urns. This dusty one says 'Augustus', so I'll give a gentle knock. Is anyone in there? Can you hear me?

VOICE:
> Go away. Tourists aren't allowed. Augustus needs his rest. Leave us alone.

LARNA:

Is that Livia speaking – his wife?

VOICE:

Well, it's not Jupiter, the king of the gods, is it? What do you want?

LARNA:

We're 'Live from the Crypt' hoping to meet you and Emperor Augustus.

VOICE:

Like I said, he's resting. He had a busy and demanding life, so he's very tired.

LARNA:

Yes, I've read about many of his achievements and we'd like him to tell us about them. If you are Livia Drusilla, you must be very proud of him.

LIVIA:

Of course. Starting up a massive empire takes some doing, I can tell you.

Interviews with the Ghosts of Roman Emperors

LARNA:

We would love to hear you both talk about all your amazing triumphs...

AUGUSTUS:

Who are you talking to, dear?

LIVIA:

Someone who wants us to talk to them.

LARNA:

Not just to me – to millions of people around the world. And we're hoping to bring along some of the other Roman ghosts from the mausoleum.

LIVIA:

We see enough of that lot. Some of them are completely outrageous.

AUGUSTUS:

Most of them were related to me and came to a grisly end, apparently. When power is given to the wrong person, it never ends well.

LIVIA:
After Augustus died (ironically in August, the month named after him), he was declared to be a god and we all worshipped him.

AUGUSTUS:
That's what I call promotion.

Interviews with the Ghosts of Roman Emperors

LIVIA:

Not bad for a guy just five feet tall, with gallstones, dirty teeth and always worried about his health.

AUGUSTUS:

Which reminds me, I need to go to the spa before I go anywhere to chat.

LIVIA:

In that case, we'll show up when we're ready. We Romans take our baths very seriously. Being ghosts, we tend to get very dusty and covered in cobwebs.

LARNA:

We look forward to seeing you on set all nice and sparkling! Please come as soon as you can – the world is waiting. In the meantime, it's back to the studio.

MISH:

(Back on the sofa) Well, that all looks very promising and we hope to bring this world-exclusive interview to you just as soon as they appear on the sofa.

JONTY:

Brilliant. I can't wait to ask Augustus about having such power at his fingertips. It must be awesome to be in charge of a huge Empire. He could have whatever he wanted – the best food, the finest wine, staying up past his bedtime...

MISH:

So what would you ask him exactly?

JONTY:

Whether his wine was always served at Rome temperature. See what I did there?

MISH:

I think we should try to be respectful, Jonty. No inappropriate jokes. If we upset any emperors on this programme we could be executed. It happened a lot.

JONTY:

I'll be careful, Mish. Then the first Roman Emperor's ghost might be keen to spook to us. See what I did there?

Interviews with the Ghosts of Roman Emperors

MISH:

Moving on... we need to set the scene so our viewers know what kind of world Augustus came into.

JONTY:

Sure – so, before he and the Empress join us here on the *Live from the Crypt* sofa, let's take a look at our plasma screen storyboard to remind us of how the Roman Empire began under Augustus...

Interviews with the Ghosts of Roman Emperors

45 BC: JULIUS CAESAR BECOMES THE FIRST DICTATOR OF ROME — THE SUPREME RULER.

"WATCH IT, YOU LOT, I'M THE MEGA-BOSS AROUND HERE."

"I SO HATE IT WHEN THIS HAPPENS."

HE LASTS A YEAR BEFORE HE IS ASSASSINATED.

Interviews with the Ghosts of Roman Emperors

Behind the Scenes

BINTI:

There's still no sign of Augustus' or Livia's ghosts. As the director, I'm in a panic. We won't have a programme if they don't show up soon.

KEV:

The infrared camera isn't picking up any images anywhere.

BINTI:

We'll have to go to a commercial break and get someone to dress up as the ghosts. As you do hair and make-up, Mandy... make yourself look like Livia.

MANDY:

Really? You want me to look like an empress?

BINTI:

Just find an old sheet and cover yourself in talc. Livia was in her late eighties.

MANDY:

(Offended) I can't do that. Anyway, wouldn't that be wrong?

BINTI:

You're right, Mandy – Kev will have to do it. Make him look like an old Roman emperor the colour of ash.

KEV:

I always thought working on TV would be glamorous. How wrong could I be?

Interviews with the Ghosts of Roman Emperors

BINTI:

We'll have to play for time. Bring in that professor of classics who did our research. Meanwhile, tell Larna to hurry with the ghosts.

MANDY:

They'll need a lot of blusher and lippy – or they'll look like washed-out ancient relics under the lights.

KEV:

That's just what they are, Mandy. This is reality TV, not glitzy-glam tinsel town.

BINTI:

Yikes, I've just had a signal in my headphones. We've got ten seconds till our sofa goes live around the world.

KEV:

But I haven't got any images coming through.

BINTI:

Cut to the sofa. Quick – Mish and Jonty, stand by.

MISH:

What do we say?

LIVE FROM THE CRYPT

KEV:

Seven seconds.

BINTI:

Make something up. Anything. Keep talking till someone shows up.

JONTY:

I can't waffle for long.

MISH:

You usually do.

KEV:

Three seconds... two... one...

MISH:

Welcome back to *Live From the Crypt*, where we're close to the famous Mausoleum of Augustus in Rome.

JONTY:

And where, any minute now, we hope the ghost of Emperor Augustus himself will be joining us on the sofa... just as soon as he and the empress appear.

Interviews with the Ghosts of Roman Emperors

We hope. Possibly. Perhaps. Maybe. With luck. Soon. Please. Er... Um...

MISH:

But in the meantime, we are joined by Professor Barbitium, who is an expert in the history of ancient civilisations and has plenty of interesting things to tell us.

PROFESSOR:

(Rushing on in a panic) Have I? I wasn't expecting this. I'm in the middle of studying fragments from an ancient Roman mosaic of Emperor Augustus.

JONTY:

Then just relax and calmly tell us about him, without going to pieces... like his mosaic. See what I did there?

MISH:

I'm sure the professor has serious things to tell us, Jonty. Is it true Augustus was the nephew of the great Julius Caesar?

PROFESSOR:

Indeed. When he was born in 63 BC, Augustus was called Gaius Octavius but known just as Octavian. After his uncle's death, he took the name 'Augustus Caesar', which means 'serene' or 'exalted'.

JONTY:

Like others born in August, the month named after him. My birthday is August.

PROFESSOR:

Maybe not all August babies show such qualities. Now, you have to remember the Roman world was in turmoil after Julius Caesar was brutally killed. After all, he had been the most powerful man in the world. The Senate made him dictator for life and he ruled like a king. He made many changes to Rome and even changed the calendar to a new one with 365 days and a leap year.

JONTY:

So from then on his days were numbered!

PROFESSOR:

In a sense. Some people felt Julius Caesar was just

Interviews with the Ghosts of Roman Emperors

too powerful and a threat to the Roman Republic. His rivals began plotting against him.

MISH:

Especially the senator Cassius and his brother-in-law Brutus.

PROFESSOR:

Yes, they and a group of others attacked and killed Caesar in the Theatre of Pompey in Rome on the fateful 15th March, known as the Ides of March. He was stabbed twenty-three times.

JONTY:
> Ouch – I bet that hurt.

PROFESSOR:
> It certainly caused an uproar and Rome was in a dangerous state until the new leader stamped his mark and eventually became emperor, bringing in a much more stable period in Roman history.

JONTY:
> I suppose all those Roman soldiers had to keep the peace.

PROFESSOR:
> Augustus gave all his soldiers a pay rise and rewarded them well for stopping any plots or riots. His army of personal bodyguards was made-up of 4,500 soldiers to protect him. He wasn't going to go the same way as Uncle Julius and it's hardly surprising everyone was keen to keep the peace from then on.

MISH:
> So Augustus was known for being a strong military ruler?

Interviews with the Ghosts of Roman Emperors

PROFESSOR:
Yes, but he was also a keen supporter of the arts. He ordered many sculptures from artists, particularly to show himself and create a strong and mighty image of him as emperor. By and large, it worked. Romans seemed to like him.

MISH:
He must have been a welcome change from all that fighting, slavery, torture and grisly goings-on under Julius Caesar.

PROFESSOR:
I'm sure. Apparently, Julius Caesar once sold the entire population of a region in Gaul (now France). 53,000 people were captured and sent to cruel slave dealers. Punishments and tortures for slaves and others could be brutal and bloody.

JONTY:
There's no need to go into details – I'm very squeamish.

PROFESSOR:
Crassus, who was a Roman general and supporter of Julius Caesar, was called the richest man

in Rome. Even he came to a gruesome end. Apparently, enemies poured molten gold down his throat because of his thirst for wealth. Bubbling gold scorched his tonsils and sizzled his stomach.

JONTY:

Please stop... I feel sick. Sorry about this...
(runs off, revolting noises)

MISH:

In that case, we'd better move on to our next item... whatever it is.

BINTI:

(Through headphones) Go to a commercial break. Where's Larna? Hurry up with the ghosts – where are they? And will someone get Jonty's head out of that bucket?

KEV:

Cue commercial break: three, two, one...

Interviews with the Ghosts of Roman Emperors

Commercial break

Interviews with the Ghosts of Roman Emperors

Live from the Crypt is brought to you by SCARED (Supreme Caesars and Roman Emperor Despots), the company with a fearsome reputation. When it comes to ultimate power, SCARED insists 'There's no place like Rome'.

Are you missing out on the latest news and gossip?

Do you need to know who's who and what's what in Rome?

Are you dying to know your horoscope? Then you need to get a local newspaper – invented by the Ancient Romans.

Interviews with the Ghosts of Roman Emperors

Read all about it...
in the Acta Diurna
(that means 'Daily Acts')
– the very first public newspaper.

Find out about upcoming events,
the latest gladiator games and
where to get bargain slaves
in this daily announcement
of notices.

No, you can't have your own copy
delivered because
a) there are no letterboxes
b) there are no deliveries
c) Acta Diurna only comes carved
in stone on message boards
around the Forum in Rome.

First published in 59 BC and edited
by Julius Caesar when he was a
Roman general. Headline:
Julius Sees A Great Opportunity!

LIVE FROM THE CRYPT

Bored of watching gladiators fight?

Fed-up of all the gossip about crazy emperors?

Looking for something to do on long summer Italian nights?

Then why not try a great new invention: a BOOK?

Interviews with the Ghosts of Roman Emperors

Yes, the first bound books, invented in ancient Rome, become widely used by the first century AD.

Written pages of papyrus (parchment first invented by Egyptians) are stitched together to make a book called a codex. No more clumsy rolls of scroll, chunky stone tablets or tiny scraps of writing means you can now read much more at once, and so easily — just turn a page and read both sides! Ideal for reading about all the latest ghastly stories of scary Roman Emperors.

Beware — page CCCLXXXVIII could be tricky to find!

HUNGRY?
DYING FOR A SNACK?
NEED TO EAT IN A HURRY?
TOO BUSY TO BOIL YOUR OWN FLAMINGO WITH DATES?

THEN WHY NOT TRY FAST FOOD, INVENTED BY THE ROMANS?

YES, FAST FOOD RESTAURANTS, KNOWN AS THERMOPOLIA, ARE OUT THERE ON THE STREETS OF ANCIENT ROME. SO, JUST GRAB A HOT SNACK FROM YOUR FAVOURITE THERMOPOLIUM, WHERE YOU COULD ALSO FIND CHEESE DIPPED IN HONEY OR FISHY GARUM (A SPECIAL ROMAN FISH SAUCE — IDEAL TO SPICE UP YOUR PORRIDGE).

Interviews with the Ghosts of Roman Emperors

Do you lose track of time?

Not sure when things are going to happen?

Keep forgetting birthdays? Then you need the latest Roman invention — a calendar.

Yes, the first 12-month calendar was first created by an ancient Roman king and later upgraded by Julius Caesar (the Julian Calendar of 46 BC). This is the first calendar based on the movement of the sun rather than the moon, with a full 365 days. Hurry — get yours while stocks last and get a few extra days free... in time for the first ever Christmas!

WARNING: THE FOLLOWING ADVERTISEMENT IS IN VERY BAD TASTE... LITERALLY.

ARE YOU LOOKING FOR THAT DAZZLING WHITE SMILE? DO YOU NEED A MOUTHWASH TO MAKE YOUR TEETH SPARKLE WITH A BRILLIANT SHINE? DO YOU LONG FOR A CLEANER, WHITER TOGA? THEN YOU NEED OUR EXTRA-SPECIAL ROMAN DETERGENT AND CLEANSER: PEE.

YES, ANCIENT ROMAN URINE HAS MANY AMAZING USES — THAT'S WHY POTS ON STREET CORNERS ARE FOR YOUR CONVENIENCE. JUST MAKE A DEPOSIT AND WEE'LL DO THE REST! URINE MAKES A GREAT ROMAN MOUTHWASH AND IT'S ALSO A KEY INGREDIENT IN LAUNDRIES CALLED FULLONICA. COLLECTED URINE IS POURED INTO VATS OF DIRTY CLOTHES, THEN WORKERS STOMP ON THE MIXTURE TO MAKE SURE THOSE PESKY STAINS ARE DISSOLVED BY THE WEE DROPS OF AMMONIA (ACTING LIKE BLEACH).

Interviews with the Ghosts of Roman Emperors

Get your clothes WIDDLE WHITE at our fizzingly fabulous FULLONICUM (just by the public piddle-orium). You're-in for a wee treat!

Roman urine also treats sores, burns and scorpion stings. Stale urine is especially useful for nappy rash. (Please don't try this at home – or anywhere else for that matter!)

Interviews with the Ghosts of Roman Emperors

In a nutshell

MISH:

Welcome back. We're still waiting for Emperor Augustus and Empress Livia to appear. Apparently they were feeling hungry so popped out to find a thermopolium.

JONTY:

I hope they don't bring back a boiled ostrich or stuffed sow's udders. Apparently they were Roman delicacies, together with the occasional dormouse.

MISH:

Let's move on. While we're waiting for them to arrive, we'll go back to our Special Correspondent who has been given a real challenge tonight.

JONTY:

Yes, Duncan has the tricky task in *Live from the Crypt* to make a big subject as simple and short as possible – 'In a nutshell'.

MISH:

Not only does he have to keep us engaged, but he must also give us basic facts in under a minute.

JONTY:

Luckily, Duncan has been joined again by Professor Barbitium to explain some Roman history. Over to you, Duncan, and good luck...

DUNCAN:

Yes, welcome to 'In a nutshell' and welcome back to Professor Barbitium.

Interviews with the Ghosts of Roman Emperors

PROFESSOR:

I'm happy to be back and to explain some ancient information in a nutshell.

DUNCAN:

Can you start by just reminding us how the Roman empire took off and what life was like for Romans under the rule of Emperor Augustus?

PROFESSOR:

Well, of course, life was often grim and short for ordinary peasants all through history. Roman citizens were divided into two main classes: the plebeians and the patricians. The patricians were the wealthy upper-class people. Everyone else was considered a plebeian.

DUNCAN:

Known as plebs. So they were just bog-standard commoners, right?

PROFESSOR:

Yes, but there was a third class under them: slaves. Around one third of the people living in Rome could

have been slaves. Most slaves were people captured in wars. As the Roman Empire grew, soldiers captured slaves from lands they conquered. Slave traders and pirates also captured people from foreign lands and brought them to Rome. Children of slaves also became slaves. Sometimes criminals or people in debt sold themselves into slavery just to get a job.

DUNCAN:

I guess life as a slave in Rome could be tough.

PROFESSOR:

It all depended on the owner. Some slaves had to do hard labour in mines or on farms. There were two main types of slaves: public and private. Public slaves were owned by the Roman government. They might work on public buildings or in the emperor's mines. Private slaves were owned by households as basic servants. Some slave owners looked after their slaves well, others could be cruel.

DUNCAN:

So, if I were a slave, would I ever be able to become free and live normally?

Interviews with the Ghosts of Roman Emperors

PROFESSOR:

You might be able to save enough to buy your freedom. Some owners would free their slaves after many years of good service. Freed slaves were considered Roman citizens, but couldn't hold public office.

DUNCAN:

I wouldn't fancy being a Roman slave. I bet it was more fun being an emperor.

PROFESSOR:

That depends. Many of them were so twitchy about plots to kill them that they couldn't rest. And they were forever stressed about who would take over from them. If an emperor didn't have a son, he would often adopt one but the struggle to keep power would sometimes end in murder, wars and utter chaos.

DUNCAN:

It's like that in our TV office! So, in a nutshell, can you tell us just a few key facts about the Roman empire?

PROFESSOR:

I'll try – here goes... Rome was the capital city of the largest empire in the ancient world. After centuries of power, the Roman empire itself began in 27 BC when Octavian became Emperor Augustus. The empire finally fell after constant enemy attacks some five hundred years later in 476 AD. In all that time, many areas were taken over by Rome, especially in Europe and north Africa.

DUNCAN:

Including Britain. The Romans invaded the British Isles and stayed for centuries, didn't they?

PROFESSOR:

They managed to conquer much of the islands, and eventually left around 400 AD. They certainly left their mark and caused many battles along the way.

DUNCAN:

But more about that later. In the meantime, it's time for me to thank you, Professor Barbitium, for helping to explain some basics of Roman history

Interviews with the Ghosts of Roman Emperors

in a nutshell in under a minute. So, while I go and give my brain a rest, let's take a look at the next clip of the reign of Emperor Augustus...

Emperor Augustus

63 BC: GAIUS OCTAVIUS THURINUS (OCTAVIAN) IS BORN IN VELLETRI, 20 MILES FROM ROME.

"I AM ATIA, JULIUS CAESAR'S NIECE."

"I AM A GOVERNOR IN THE ROMAN REPUBLIC. MY BABY SON WILL BE GREAT."

"MY DADDY DIED AND I WANT TO BE LIKE HIM – EXCEPT ALIVE."

THE YOUNG OCTAVIAN SPENDS MUCH TIME WITH GRANNY JULIA, THE SISTER OF JULIUS CAESAR.

Interviews with the Ghosts of Roman Emperors

"YOU'RE MY THIRD WIFE BUT WE'LL NEVER GET DIVORCED, DARLING."

"I KNOW, BECAUSE I WANT MY LITTLE SON TIBERIUS TO BE THE NEXT EMPEROR, TEE HEE."

38 BC: Emperor Augustus marries Livia Drusilla.

"I HAVE REIGNED FOR 40 YEARS AND MADE ROME GREAT. JUST LOOK AT MY FORUM. WHAT COULD POSSIBLY GO WRONG?"

"I FOUND ROME OF CLAY; I LEAVE IT TO YOU OF MARBLE. HAVE I PLAYED MY PART WELL? THEN APPLAUD ME AS I EXIT."

Emperor Augustus dies in 14 AD and is named a god.

65

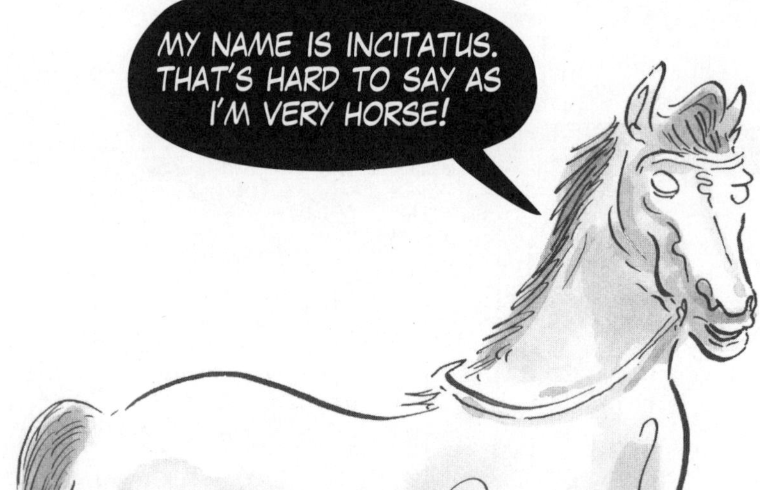

Interviews with the Ghosts of Roman Emperors

Spot the emperor

JONTY:

Hello again – and while we're still waiting for Emperor Augustus and Empress Livia to join us on the sofa, we've asked Professor Barbitium to join us again and to put Mish and me to the test with a quick quiz.

MISH:

Yes, and we haven't had time to revise so it's all a bit scary. Neither Jonty nor I have seen the questions in advance.

PROFESSOR:

Neither have I. I was literally grabbed ten seconds ago to come back and throw some random questions your way to see if you can name the emperor from the clues I give you. You have a one in five chance of picking the right ruler.

JONTY:

That's because we're sticking to the first five emperors. I'm not sure I can even name them in the right order. I know the first one was Augustus.

MISH:

Next up was Tiberius. I'm pretty sure the next after him was Caligula.

JONTY:

Then it was Claudius and wasn't Nero number five?

PROFESSOR:

Correct – but no points for that. So, first question – which emperor was said to adore his horse so much that he fed it gold? At least, oats mixed with gold flakes.

Interviews with the Ghosts of Roman Emperors

JONTY:

I have that for breakfast most mornings. What do you think, Mish?

MISH:

I think I can guess because I know there's a bit of a legend about Caligula planning to make his horse some kind of an official. Would it be Caligula?

PROFESSOR:

Correct. Caligula's horse was called Incitatus and there are many stories about it being very pampered with purple blankets, a collar full of jewels and a stable made of marble. True or not, the only stable thing about Caligula was his horse!

JONTY:

Nice joke! Didn't he also murder a lot of his own family?

PROFESSOR:

That was my next question. Spot the emperor who was said to have killed his cousin and adopted son, several of his in-laws, and even his own grandmother.

JONTY:

What a family barbecue that turned out to be!

MISH:

So the answer must be Caligula.

PROFESSOR:

Correct. However did you guess? Try this one. Spot the emperor who banished his daughter to a remote island to punish her for bad behaviour.

JONTY:

That makes a change from being sent to the naughty step! Can you give a clue?

PROFESSOR:

This emperor became a Roman god after his death.

MISH:

That's Augustus – we've already heard that the Romans worshipped him.

PROFESSOR:

Correct. So which emperor married his own niece

Interviews with the Ghosts of Roman Emperors

as his fourth wife? Here's a clue: he began the Roman invasion of Britain.

MISH:

Ah, did he happen to speak with a stammer and walk with a limp?

PROFESSOR:

Indeed. And that fourth wife of his was bad news for him and Rome.

MISH:

Could it be Claudius?

PROFESSOR:

Correct. He tried his best but then his fourth wife ensured her son took over, who turned out to be quite a villain. We call him the last of the Julio-Claudian dynasty and he was one of the worst emperors ever.

JONTY:

The others haven't sounded too brilliant so far! You must be talking about Nero.

PROFESSOR:

Correct. He apparently wanted to be an opera singer and one of his performances was so shocking that pregnant women in the audience began giving birth in the amphitheatre – probably straining not to laugh!

MISH:

Why didn't people just walk out if his singing was so bad?

PROFESSOR:

No one was allowed to leave for many hours – not even for a comfort break. But that was nothing compared to the torture he kept for Christians, who were persecuted very cruelly towards the end of his reign.

JONTY:

I don't want to hear the grisly details, I'm squeamish about executions.

PROFESSOR:

Talking of executions, spot the emperor who executed people by having them thrown from a cliff into the sea while he watched. If anyone survived the fall,

Interviews with the Ghosts of Roman Emperors

soldiers waiting below in boats would finish them off with boat-hooks.

MISH:

You must be talking about Tiberius – he's the only one left.

PROFESSOR:

Correct – the emperor whose adopted grandson plotted against him. So the charming Tiberius had young Drusus Caesar thrown into a dungeon where he starved to death, after trying to eat the stuffing from his bed.

JONTY:

Yuck! We would just like to warn viewers that eating your mattress is not to be advised and doesn't count as one of your 'five-a-day', despite the high-fibre.

MISH:

Moving on... I've just heard in my earpiece that Tiberius will be joining us later and he's not happy about the negative stories told about him, so he's coming to show just how charming he was.

PROFESSOR:

I've never heard 'Tiberius' and 'charming' in the same sentence – but I'm pleased to say you've both scored several points in 'Spot the emperor'.

JONTY:

Thank you, Professor Barbitium, and while on the subject of the second Roman Emperor Tiberius, let's take a look at the next clip on the giant screen about his reign and how he came to a rather nasty end...

Interviews with the Ghosts of Roman Emperors

Interviews with the Ghosts of Roman Emperors

"I LOVE WATCHING EXECUTIONS FROM THE CLIFFTOPS!"

TIBERIUS'S BEHAVIOUR BECOMES MONSTROUS, TOO...

TIBERIUS DIES IN BED.

"OUCH, I'VE TORN MY SHOULDER... I'M FAINTING."

37 AD: AT THE AGE OF 79, TIBERIUS TRIES TO THROW A JAVELIN AT A CEREMONY.

CAN YOU GUESS WHAT REALLY HAPPENED?

79

Interviews with the Ghosts of Roman Emperors

Spin the news

ALEEMA:
Welcome to 'Spin the news', where I spin a dial for the news headlines for a mystery year *(spins a dial which stops at 37)*. AD 37. That was yet another scary year in Ancient Rome and we're about to find out why from a ghost who has just appeared...

GHOST:
I'm not buried here but I keep my eye on what's going on. I've come to stop any bad stories being told about me.

ALEEMA:

Were you one of the first emperors of Rome, by any chance?

GHOST:

Of course but I'm not saying who yet. You'll have to guess. But that year you mentioned was special for me.

ALEEMA:

AD 37 – the year Tiberius died and Caligula took over. So which one are you?

GHOST:

Neither – but I can tell you plenty about them both. The Ides of March was something of a bad omen for us Caesars.

ALEEMA:

Ah, the 15th March. Why was that date important for Romans?

GHOST:

That date is the 74th day in our Roman calendar, the day for religious events and our special day of the year for settling debts. It seemed to be the date for murders, too. In fact, they reckon Emperor Tiberius almost died on 15th March but recovered and was promptly murdered the following day.

ALEEMA:

So, elderly Tiberius injured himself and lay on his deathbed in a coma, right?

GHOST:

And Caligula took his ring and was about to become the next emperor when Tiberius woke up. Caligula was horrified the top job was slipping from his grasp.

ALEEMA:

Wasn't he pleased the emperor was getting better?

GHOST:

Don't be daft, this is Rome. Power is everything! Caligula simply sent his chief guard to tend to Tiberius. That meant getting a nice big pillow and pushing it down on the old man's head to finish him off. Job done. Being Tiberius's grand-nephew and adopted grandson, Caligula was duly hailed the third emperor.

LIVE FROM THE CRYPT

ALEEMA:

Was it a smooth changeover and a happy time?

GHOST:

Don't be daft, this was Rome. There were all sorts of squabbles and jostlings for power, with a few murders thrown in. Within six months, Caligula was very sick. He'd probably been poisoned so he got very stressy and started to kill off anyone around him who might be a threat. It all got pretty nasty, apparently.

ALEEMA:

Were you there? Did you know Tiberius, by any chance?

GHOST:

Don't be daft. AD 37 was the year I was born. On 15th December. I only just remember Uncle Caligula as he was killed when I was about four. They all said he was completely bonkers. Some said I took after him!

ALEEMA:

I've just worked out you must be Nero. Many said you were even worse than your Uncle Caligula.

Interviews with the Ghosts of Roman Emperors

NERO:

How dare you! As the fifth Roman Emperor, I was absolutely marvellous.

ALEEMA:

Well, that's for viewers to judge later when we see your story. In the meantime, we'd better check out some more about your scary Uncle Caligula in the next clip. The year AD 37 was obviously quite a year, especially when Caligula became emperor. Be warned, look away now if you're of a nervous disposition...

Interviews with the Ghosts of ROMAN EMPERORS

How nice to meet you

MISH:

Welcome back to the *Live from the Crypt* sofa with me, Mish Varma.

JONTY:

And me, Jonty Yardley – and we're very excited, aren't we, Mish?

MISH:

Excited and privileged because finally, at last, our special guests tonight have just arrived on set and will be joining us on the sofa any minute now.

JONTY:

Yes, the ghosts of Emperor Augustus, the first Roman Emperor, and his third wife, Empress Livia, have just appeared beside us. Welcome to you both.

LIVIA:

My husband is a god so don't forget it. Respect and worship at all times.

AUGUSTUS:

Livia has always tried to protect and advise me. It's very touching, even though she can be ruthless. Don't upset her.

LIVIA:

It's for your own good, dear. I tried to be a proper Roman wife by cooking and making clothes, as well as making sure I got my own way. I was determined that my son Tiberius would become the next emperor – at any cost.

AUGUSTUS:

You were very ambitious, dear. As tough as old caligae boots.

Interviews with the Ghosts of Roman Emperors

LIVIA:

You could be pretty tough, too. Mind you, you were forever fussing about your health, constantly taking hot saltwater baths for rheumatism.

AUGUSTUS:

Baths are what made Romans great. There's nothing like a good soak. It did me good. After all, I outlived my two grandsons and lived to a good age.

LIVIA:

True, probably because of all the layers you wore in winter: four tunics and a heavy toga, as well as an undershirt, a woollen chest-protector, and wraps for your shins and thighs.

AUGUSTUS:

Shhh, dear, too much information. I get chilly, that's all.

JONTY:

Even gods have to wrap up warm, it seems.

LIVIA:

The heat didn't suit Augustus, either. In summer he slept with the doors of his bedroom open and had someone fan him all night.

MISH:

The first Roman air-con! I thought Italians enjoyed the heat of summer.

LIVIA:

Augustus couldn't endure the sun even in winter and never walked in the open air without wearing a broad-brimmed hat, even at home. Bless him.

JONTY:

Despite all the strains of running an empire, you both lived long lives and had a long marriage. That was unusual for the Roman emperors who followed you.

LIVIA:

Augustus had previous wives and he divorced them. I was his favourite and our marriage lasted LII years.

Interviews with the Ghosts of Roman Emperors

JONTY:
LII?

MISH:
Ah yes, that's fifty-two.

LIVIA:
A shame we didn't make another two years, as that's what he called me.

JONTY:
Augustus called you fifty-four?

MISH:
No, Jonty – keep up. Fifty-four is LIV in Roman numerals. Short for Livia.

JONTY:
I find Roman numerals confusing. Didn't you ever think about replacing Roman numerals with real numbers?

AUGUSTUS:
Not on my watch.

JONTY:

I didn't think Romans had watches.

MISH:

It was a joke, Jonty.

JONTY:

Ah, I get it now. Very funny. Did you hear about the Roman soldier who was branded with his ID number: 51-6-500?

LIVIA:

That must have made him rather cross.

JONTY:

Cross? He was LI-VI-D. Get it? That's a Roman numerals joke, by the way.

AUGUSTUS:

I wish you hadn't bothered. Even though English has Latin roots, I've never really understood your language. Great-uncle Julius Caesar tried to conquer Britain but I could never be bothered with the place or its languages.

Interviews with the Ghosts of Roman Emperors

LIVIA:

He tried a couple of times, didn't he?

AUGUSTUS:

I was just a boy at the time. In 55 BC, then the following year, Roman soldiers invaded Britain but gave it up as a bad job. We wanted the iron and tin but the locals were an uncivilised bunch.

JONTY:

You ought to see them today!

AUGUSTUS:

For the second invasion in 54 BC, we sent 628 ships, five legions and 2,000 cavalry. It was more than an afternoon's picnic, you know.

MISH:

You might be interested to know that Livia's grandson sent the next invasion, which lasted four hundred years. In fact, let's pause right there to take a look at when Emperor Claudius conquered Britain, which must have seemed like a piece of cake for him compared to coping with his notorious fourth wife.

JONTY:
> Yes, be aware of what's coming next. There's bound to be more murder, scary plots and yet more people with the same names who then changed them to yet more of the same names. Why did Romans keep doing that? I can never work out who's who and who's someone else.

MISH:
> Emperors often gave their children the same or similar names, then remarried relatives with almost identical names. That's why it can get confusing.

JONTY:
> Or what you might call Maximus Confusicus.

MISH:
> Absoluticus!

AUGUSTUS:
> That's Ridiculus!

LIVIA:
> I suppose our family gatherings could be a bit of a nightmare with so many Neros and Tiberiuses or Agrippinas and Caesars.

Interviews with the Ghosts of Roman Emperors

JONTY:
Maybe that's why you kept killing each other. Let's find out more as we return to the giant screen for the next clip about the rise and fall of Emperor Claudius...

Interviews with the Ghosts of Roman Emperors

Forecast

JONTY:

While we're waiting for some other ghost guests to join us, we can take a look at the forecast and get the outlook from Gail Forse. What sort of conditions can Britain expect as Emperor Claudius leads his invading army over from France, known as Gaul, to cross the Channel?

GAIL:

Well, Jonty – spectacular conditions are on the way... as powerful forces spread up through many regions from the south east, bringing major stormy

LIVE FROM THE CRYPT

events. Under the leadership of General Plautius, four Roman legions hit the Kent coast and sweep northwards. The winds of change are violent and last a blustery thirty years as Rome fights to gain control of the southern part of the island. Where two fronts meet in eastern areas, there will be a severe warning of rising temperatures, a hail of blows and violent outbursts.

There are even rumours that when Emperor Claudius first set foot in Britain he asked his general what weather he should expect. The answer? 'Hail, Caesar, of course!'

The Romans call this land 'Britannia', which means 'the land of tin'. They begin to spread in all directions, building forts, roads and towns, as well as digging for tin and other minerals. Their garrison town in the east is Camulodunum (now Colchester) where the locals are very frosty. One Roman described the Britons as looking like 'wood-demons, their hair thick and shaggy like a horse's mane. Some shave their cheeks but leave a moustache that covers the whole mouth.' Welcome to Essex!

Interviews with the Ghosts of Roman Emperors

After a long period of turmoil, further clashes and the spread of Latin culture, a long settled spell will follow. Eventually, after some 400 years, the reign will begin to dry up. After a glorious summer comes the FALL of the empire, when Romans head south once more and return to Italy. And that's your forecast.

Interviews with the Ghosts of Roman Emperors

IT DOESN'T END WELL FOR BOUDICCA AND HER 200,000 WARRIORS.

THAT SHOWED THEM WHO'S BOSS!

BOUDICCA RIP

WHETHER SHE DIED OF HER WOUNDS OR FROM TAKING HER OWN LIFE, WE'LL NEVER KNOW.

ROMANS 1
BRITONS 0

Interviews with the Ghosts of Roman Emperors

Ghosts reunited

MISH:

Welcome back to the *Live from the Crypt* sofa, where we're delighted to have Emperor Augustus and Empress Livia still with us, although Augustus fell asleep watching the last clip.

JONTY:

Yes, this is 'Ghosts reunited' where we bring together ghosts who haven't met for a while, which could make for an interesting encounter.

MISH:
That's because we're about to welcome from the mausoleum behind us none other than Emperor Caligula and his fourth wife, Empress Milonia.

CALIGULA:
It's great to be here and back on show for everyone to adore me. It's awesome to meet Augustus again – my step-great-grandpa! And Livia is my great-grandma. You may kiss my hand.

LIVIA:
(Muttering) Not likely. He was a spoilt brat of a kid and he hasn't changed.

AUGUSTUS:
Don't tell me he became the emperor? I remember him as a ghastly two-year-old dressed as a soldier. My stepson Tiberius promised to make the great general Germanicus his heir, not that little nincompoop Caligula.

MILONIA
Although we only had four years in office, we made Rome truly great again.

Interviews with the Ghosts of Roman Emperors

CALIGULA:
True. I got Rome really great again. I'm the best ever – a winner, never a loser.

JONTY:
Being assassinated by your own people sounds like a loser to me.

AUGUSTUS:
And to me.

LIVIA:
Me too. I'm sure you didn't learn to be so ghastly from my sweet son, Tiberius.

CALIGULA:
There was nothing sweet about Uncle Tiberius (also weirdly my step-grandpa). To be honest, we got rid of him as he was getting sick and old. I also hated him.

MILONIA:
He had to go to make room for a better emperor.

LIVIA:
You killed my son, Tiberius? How dare you.

CALIGULA:

He made fun of me. They all made fun of me because I'm just a bit hairy.

MILONIA:

Don't mention goats whatever you do.

JONTY:

You've got to be kidding!

CALIGULA:

If anyone mentioned goats in front of me, I had them executed. It made me furious. I'd torture anyone who mentioned hair – and anyone who didn't.

AUGUSTUS:

So you've got hairy legs, so what?

MILONIA:

So did your horse Incitatus and you adored him, dear.

CLAUDIUS:

That's different. We were very close. In fact, he was my nearest neigh-bour! Ha!

Interviews with the Ghosts of Roman Emperors

MISH:

Moving on... Is it true you even had statues beheaded, replacing their heads with your own, declaring yourself to be a god?

CALIGULA:

Fake news. Fake news. But yes.

JONTY:

I read somewhere you told the public they had to worship you.

MILONIA:

When you're a god like Caligula, you can do that. He often dressed as the Roman god Jupiter, too, or the goddess Venus. It made breakfast very interesting.

LIVIA:

No wonder they got rid of you.

MILONIA:

It was terrible. On 24th January in the year 41 AD we were watching a private performance of a play and suddenly they attacked my husband. They then

came for our daughter and me. I stuck out my neck and dared them to harm me, too.

AUGUSTUS:

And did they?

MILONIA:

Yes. They finished us all off. I was furious.

CALIGULA:

But we were never losers. Never losers. We'll go down in history as the greatest leaders of all time – and you all know it. We made Rome great again. Really great. Really, really great.

AUGUSTUS:

So why couldn't you bear to let people smile at you or make goat jokes? I could always take a joke against me – that's the sign of someone who is wise enough to shrug off such things. You must have felt very insecure.

CALIGULA:

Just look at me. Do I look insecure? I'm the greatest emperor ever.

Interviews with the Ghosts of Roman Emperors

MISH:

A Roman historian called Suetonius wrote this about you: 'Caligula was horribly pale, had the face of an old man with gloomy, deep-set eyes. His head was deformed and bald, except for a few scanty hairs. His neck was covered with bristles. He had thin legs and enormous feet.'

CALIGULA:

Send for this Suetonius immediately and have him thrown to the lions.

LIVIA:

So, Milonia, whatever attracted you to your ugly but very rich husband?

MILONIA:

We both loved gold and wild parties. There's nothing better than spreading gold coins over our palace and dancing on them in bare feet. He loved that.

CALIGULA:

And don't forget I built a temple dedicated to me with a life-sized golden statue of me inside.

Each day it was dressed in whatever I was wearing. Rome's richest citizens would make offerings to me there, with gifts of flamingos, peacocks and exotic creatures. That's why Milonia couldn't resist me.

MILONIA:

And your sense of fun, darling. Do you remember the ceremony when you were sacrificing a bull to the gods? Instead of hitting it over the head with a mallet, you turned and bashed the priest. It was so hilarious.

JONTY:

It sounds violent to me. No wonder the Senate voted to erase you from Roman history after your death. They ordered the destruction of your statues and public inscriptions, and your coins were melted down. You were despised.

CALIGULA:

Rubbish. I was certainly never despised by my horse. Had he been on the Senate as I once suggested, he'd have voted NEIGH! See what I did there? If you don't laugh, I'll have you executed.

Interviews with the Ghosts of Roman Emperors

MISH:

That's almost as bad as your jokes, Jonty.

JONTY:

Thanks a lot, at least I'm not an evil tyrant. On that reassuring note, we thank our guests for the time being and leave 'Ghosts reunited' to return to the giant plasma screen to see what became of Caligula's little sister. Stay tuned for the next instalment to see how scariness can run in the family...

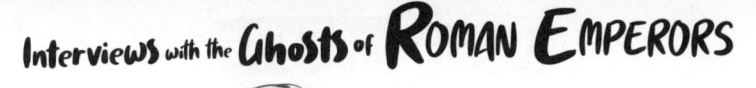

Interviews with the Ghosts of Roman Emperors

I'm a Cel-emperor... Get Me Out of Here!

DUNCAN:

Welcome to 'I'm A Cel-emperor... Get Me Out of Here!', where we're down to our last six contestants. Tonight's vote will decide the winner from all the emperors and empresses who took part.

ALEEMA:

Yes, we're down to three couples who, although once married, were often at each other's throats. So we'll be setting them some scary tasks to see how they deal with a stressful challenge together, despite hating one

another. Then the phone lines will open for viewers to cast their votes for the emperor or empress to be crowned Celebrity Caesar of Imperial Rome.

DUNCAN:

So let's find out what grisly challenges await our contestants in the amphitheatre arena. And you know what that means?

ALEEMA:

Of course I know what that means. Arena means 'sand' because that's what's on the floor to soak up the blood from all the injured gladiators and Roman prisoners savaged by wild animals for the amusement of the crowd.

DUNCAN:

Thankfully, we're not expecting too much blood or too many scary gladiators tonight. We'd better get started. 'Ave Caesar! Morituri te salutant!'

ALEEMA:

That means 'Hail, Caesar! We who are about to die salute you!' It was the usual cry from gladiators before their contests in front of emperors.

Interviews with the Ghosts of Roman Emperors

DUNCAN:

First up, we have Emperor Tiberius and his third wife, now known as Julia the elder.

JULIA:

I'm not happy about the 'elder' bit. After all, I was younger than Tiberius and died before him – mainly because he sent me away, locked me up and starved me to death. Apart from that, we had a nice wedding.

TIBERIUS:

You were out of control most of the time. You were always having wild parties. Your own father, Emperor Augustus, sent you away to an island because you were so wild and outrageous.

JULIA:

I liked having a good time, that's all. I found you boring, which is probably why we never got on. I dread to think what you'll be like for our challenge as you'd always get stroppy if you didn't get your own way. Everyone hated you.

TIBERIUS:

My mother liked me – on good days. I've never got

over my very last day. There I was, lying in bed after getting injured, and I felt Caligula squeezing my gold emperor's ring off me – the symbol of Roman power. I saw him slip it on his own finger and strut about. I demanded it back... and that's the last I remember.

ALEEMA:

Well, now you're both getting on so well, let's get started with your challenge.

DUNCAN:

Yes, we have a hot tub prepared that you can both sit in together.

TIBERIUS:

That's easy enough *(climbs inside)*. We Romans like a good bath.

JULIA:

There's no water in here yet *(climbs inside)* and I don't want it too cold.

ALEEMA:

It won't be filled with water – something else is gushing down the pipe.

Interviews with the Ghosts of Roman Emperors

TIBERIUS:

It's like porridge – no, it's all wriggly and heaving around my knees.

JULIA:

Aaah, it's all pouring in and coming up to my neck. It looks like noodles.

ALEEMA:

More like spaghetti, but you didn't have that kind of pasta in your time.

DUNCAN:

Romans were proud of being clean and hygienic, what with communal toilets, public baths and the disposal of human waste in carts. But we now know the Roman Empire had many parasites. Studies have shown that tapeworms were common.

ALEEMA:

And a well-known treatment for injuries was to put maggots on the wounds. Maggots are known to clean up infected tissue.

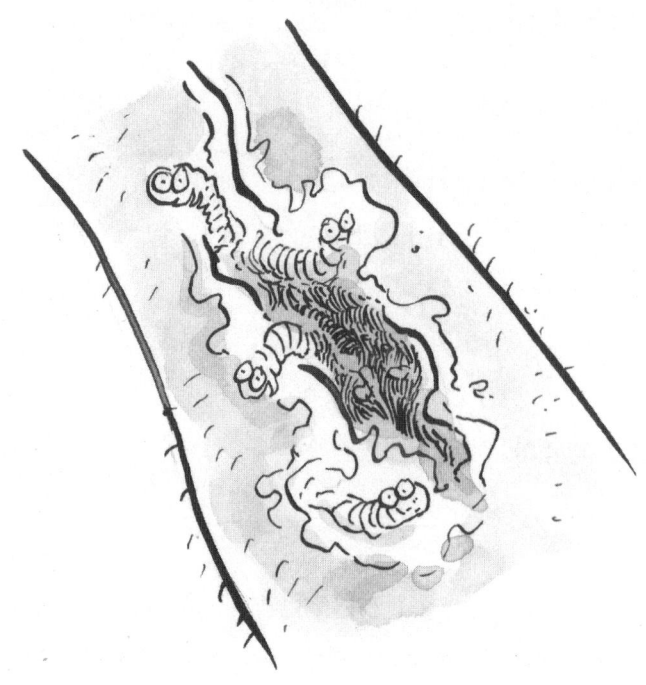

TIBERIUS:

We're up to our necks in heaving maggots and tapeworms!

DUNCAN:

And you just have to stay there without moving or arguing for one minute.

Interviews with the Ghosts of Roman Emperors

JULIA:

We've never been able to stop arguing for a full minute.

TIBERIUS:

I'll keep my mouth firmly shut. Yuk, a maggot is wiggling in my ear. Eek, I didn't keep my mouth shut and they're now squirming on my tongue...

ALEEMA:

So while we leave Emperor Tiberius and Empress Julia to sit out their challenge in silence, we now meet our next couple: Emperor Claudius and his fourth wife, Empress Agrippina.

CLAUDIUS:

I don't want anything to do with that woman – she poisoned me.

AGRIPPINA:

Where's your sense of fun, dear? You enjoyed those mushrooms... to begin with, anyway.

CLAUDIUS:

I hope you never trusted that son of yours. If Nero

became emperor after me, things would have gone really pirum figura *(pear-shaped)*.

Agrippina

Nero completely lost the plot, I'm afraid. He should never have become emperor. It didn't end well for me, I have to say.

Duncan:

Before you go into details and spoil the final video clip on Nero, let's get started with your challenge. It involves eating something gross and spitting out none of it.

Aleema:

It's making me feel sick just looking at it. So please, both take your places at the table and lift the lid of your dish. The winner will be the first to finish the whole lot.

Duncan:

You have in front of you a sea urchin – that's a little porcupine-like ocean creature seasoned with pepper and olive oil, on top of sheep brains in a grey sludge of rotting fish guts.

Interviews with the Ghosts of Roman Emperors

CLAUDIUS:

Delicious. That's garum, a Roman delicacy. It's a kind of fermented fish sauce.

AGRIPPINA:

What, no mushrooms? Fish innards smell at the best of times, but when they are left in the sun for months to mature, they can be rather strong.

DUNCAN:

You also have a goblet of gladiator's blood to wash it down, and a nice warm slice of his raw liver. Apparently such delights were prized as cures or for giving the consumer gladiatorial strength – even though the poor gladiator had just been killed.

Interviews with the Ghosts of Roman Emperors

ALEEMA:

That's so disgusting. While we leave Emperor Claudius and Empress Agrippina to gobble down their revolting slops, we now meet our final couple: Emperor Nero and his first wife, Claudia Octavia.

OCTAVIA:

I'm known as Octavia but I'm not happy being here with that monster.

NERO:

We were married, dear. You're the daughter of Emperor Claudius and my adopted sister. We're meant to be close – even though we've always despised each other. That's the trouble with the Caesar dynasty: our marriages were often planned for us. You were just thirteen and we weren't in love at all.

OCTAVIA:

How could anyone love you? Did you treat your other wives anything like the way you treated me by sending me away to an island to get rid of me? You killed my brother and you ordered guards to kill me.

NERO:

I was twenty-two and bored with you, Octavia. Killing you was Poppaea's idea. She wanted to marry me so I ordered for you to be suffocated in a hot bath and to have your head cut off. They sent your head to Poppaea. She was delighted with it. If it makes you feel any better, I later killed Poppaea in a fit of rage.

DUNCAN:

As this is a family show, we don't want to go into gory details. Enough to say, you were a very violent man. So we'll stand at a safe distance as we get started with your challenge against the clock.

ALEEMA:

Yes, you each have a sack and you simply have to step inside it.

NERO:

Are we having a sack race? Is that all?

DUNCAN:

It's more of a race to get out of the sack, before we throw you into the River Tiber which is right next to us.

Interviews with the Ghosts of Roman Emperors

OCTAVIA:

That was a punishment in Rome for anyone who killed one of their parents.

NERO:

Whoever would do such a thing?

ALEEMA:

Spoiler alert – wait till the next video clip.

DUNCAN:

The culprit would be sewn up inside the sack, together with a dog, a chicken, a monkey and a snake. They're already wriggling inside your sacks, so in you get.

OCTAVIA:

(Getting in sack)
Ouch, the chicken keeps pecking and the dog is growling.

NERO:

(Getting in sack)
I'm more worried about the screaming monkey and hissing snake.

ALEEMA:

All we do now is sew up the top of the sack and secure it with a rope.

DUNCAN:

And all you have to do is try to escape before you land in the river. Good luck.

ALEEMA:

So while we leave you to 'get out of here' before the minute is up, we can see Tiberius and Julia still squabbling among the maggots and Claudius and Agrippina slurping down urchins, brains and rotten fish sauce – while Nero and Octavia are now screaming inside their sacks as they roll down the riverbank.

DUNCAN:

It's now over to viewers at home to vote for the Roman you want to be crowned as top Celebrity Caesar of Imperial Rome.

ALEEMA:

While each of them squeals just eight words...

Interviews with the Ghosts of Roman Emperors

ALL:

I'm A Cel-emperor... Get Me Out of Here!

DUNCAN:

With their ghostly screams echoing around the streets of Rome, we'll return to the giant plasma screen to see just how dreadful Emperor Nero could be. Look away now if you are feeling delicate...

Nero

54 AD: Nero is crowned Emperor at the age of 17, after Agrippina poisons Emperor Claudius.

"Thanks, Mum."

"Your mum killed my dad."

"Who cares? Anyway, my mum is driving me mad."

"Nag, nag, nag, nag, nag..."

Nero's wife is Octavia, the daughter of Emperor Claudius.

142

Interviews with the Ghosts of Roman Emperors

59 AD: NERO THINKS HIS MOTHER IS INTERFERING TOO MUCH, SO HE TRIES TO GET RID OF HER BY SINKING HER SHIP.

"HERE, MUM, GO FOR A NICE BOAT TRIP."

"HOW NICE, DEAR."

"SOMETHING VERY FISHY IS GOING ON HERE."

SHE SURVIVES.

PLAN B: NERO SENDS ASSASSINS TO HIS MOTHER'S VILLA.

143

Interviews with the Ghosts of Roman Emperors

Who am I?

ALEEMA:

Welcome back to The Augustus Mausoleum in Rome, which is in total darkness. We're about to hear three voices coming from inside. We have already seen these ghosts but now we will only hear them. The puzzle is to work out which emperor or empress is speaking. So here goes with our first 'Who Am I?' as we listen to one of the ancient Roman ghosts talking to us from the darkness...

VOICE 1:

After my plot to kill my big brother failed, he took away all my possessions and sent me off to the remote Pontine Islands. I was stuck there with nothing to meddle with, so I was delighted when someone got rid of him and I could return to the excitement of Rome. Things got even better when my second husband died and I inherited his wealth and estates. At his funeral, people whispered that I had poisoned him just to get my hands on his money. As if I'd do such a thing. Mind you, I then married the next emperor to make sure I had a firm grip on power. When my own son tried to poison me several times and made my bedroom ceiling collapse, I was lucky to escape. When I was 43 years old, he eventually killed me and claimed he was haunted by my ghost, so he hired magicians to send my spirit away. Whooo ha ha ha! Who am I?

ALEEMA:

Just text the name of who you think that Roman might be, for your chance to win a prize. We'll give the answer shortly once the phone lines are closed. Meanwhile, here's our second mystery Roman…

Interviews with the Ghosts of Roman Emperors

VOICE 2:

I was the previous mystery guest's great-grandmother. I was known for looking stunning with a simple and severe hairstyle, based on the hairdo seen on images of the Roman goddesses. I wore a roll of hair, called a nodus in Latin, across the forehead and with the side locks pulled back to form a small bun at the neck. This hairstyle became my trademark and was popular among upper-class women in Roman society who wished to look like me. I dressed simply, not often in silk and never with fancy jewellery. My grandson became emperor after my death and had me declared a goddess. How nice. Who am I?

ALEEMA:

Once again, just text us the name for your chance to win a prize. Next up is our third and final ancient Roman, so fingers poised to text the name...

VOICE 3:

I sang and performed music and poetry – I should really have been an actor. I even encouraged the upper classes to take dancing lessons. I ordered

public games to be held every five years in Rome and I trained as an athlete myself, becoming an excellent chariot racer. In fact, I won the Olympic ten-horse chariot race, even though I fell off. They wouldn't dare let me lose! That's because I had a reputation for burning people to death in big bonfires to light up my all-night garden parties. Oh yes, and anyone else I didn't like would be dressed in animal skins and hunted by dogs to be torn apart. Such fun. But I had great style – having a thirty-metre-high bronze statue made of myself. How stunning is that? Who am I?

ALEEMA:

Hmm – tricky, perhaps. Did you manage all three names? Listen up now as Professor Barbitium gives us the answers. No more texting, lines are closed. Good luck in winning the prize: a pinch of salt. After all, Romans were said to value salt highly and sometimes used it as currency when bartering for goods.

PROFESSOR:

The first 'Who Am I?' is Empress Agrippina the Younger, mother of Nero. The second 'Who Am I?' is Livia Augustus, mother of Germanicus and

Interviews with the Ghosts of Roman Emperors

Tiberius. And our third 'Who Am I? is Nero – or, to give him his full name: Nero Claudius Caesar Augustus Germanicus.

ALEEMA:

Thank you, Professor Barbitium. Hopefully someone managed to get those right and yes, I see on the computer screen that our winner is a Mrs M Press from just outside Colchester. Very appropriate. So finally... we return to the *Live from the Crypt* sofa to conclude tonight's show.

JONTY:

Yes, welcome back as we say our farewells to our ghost guests.

MISH:

We still have Emperor Augustus and Empress Livia with us but unfortunately Caligula and Milonia stormed off in a fit of temper.

LIVIA:

It runs in the family, I'm afraid. The Caesars were a hot-tempered bunch.

AUGUSTUS:

Not me, I was always cool and calm – apart from when we first met and you sent me a long letter. I was so excited to see a kiss on the bottom.

LIVIA:

A kiss on the bottom? I'd never dream of such a thing. It was an 'X' for page ten.

AUGUSTUS:

An X looked like a kiss on the bottom of the page to me!

JONTY:

We thought we might finish with a couple of Roman limericks. Here's the first one about Livia's son.

MISH:

The exploits of Emperor Tiberius
Became very scary and serious.
When old and in bed,
He ended up dead.
The cause was guess who? How mysterious!

Interviews with the Ghosts of Roman Emperors

LIVIA:

My son could be very mysterious, I can tell you.

MISH:

At least he wasn't as bad as Emperor Nero. Listen to this one...

JONTY:

The thing about Emperor Nero,
He'll never be thought as a hero...
Getting madder and tougher,
How he made people suffer...
Marks out of ten? A round ZERO!

AUGUSTUS:

I think I could do one of those rhymes about me.

LIVIA:

Go on then, dear – go for it.

AUGUSTUS:

I'm the Caesar who's known as Augustus,
With a beautiful wife – you can trust us!
Now we're ghosts stuck at home

*In our crypt under Rome,
Stuffed in urns – so come for a chat and please dust us.*

LIVIA:

*As I'm Livia Julia Augusta,
My story is quite a blockbuster,
For I went (which seems odd)
From empress to god,
To an urn – now needing a flick of the duster!*

MISH:

Brilliant – your limericks are better than ours. But no more limericks as our time is up, so it just remains for us to ask Larna to take our guests back to their crypt.

LARNA:

Indeed, and maybe we can persuade Emperor Augustus and Empress Livia to return for another *Live from the Crypt* in 2047 to mark a special anniversary.

AUGUSTUS:

That would be splendid – which anniversary would that be?

Interviews with the Ghosts of Roman Emperors

LARNA:

Well, back in 47 AD, Emperor Claudius revived the Secular Games for three days and nights of ceremonies, sports, parties and all sorts to celebrate the eight-hundredth anniversary of the founding of Rome.

JONTY:

So why don't we do the same in 2047 to mark the 2800th anniversary?

LIVIA:

Don't you mean MMDCCC?

AUGUSTUS:

It will also be our MMX wedding anniversary.

MISH:

Wow – we could invite hundreds of Roman ghost guests to join us.

JONTY:

Make it one thousand and nine – that would make a real MIX. See what I did there?

LIVIA:

We shall make it a date. Let's mark it in our special Roman calendar, as invented by Julius Caesar.

JONTY:

I think it's amazing he invented the 365-day calendar. Apparently the very first Roman calendar was stolen from a museum in Rome. But they caught the thief and immediately sent him to prison. He got twelve months.

MISH:

Moving on... before anyone else starts telling ancient jokes. It's time for us to end tonight's live programme packed with long-dead guests now returning to their resting places.

LARNA:

So join us again for *Live from the Crypt* at the BIG anniversary to mark the founding of ancient Rome. Meanwhile, it's goodbye from us at The Augustus Mausoleum in Rome and all our ghostly guests. Goodnight!

Interviews with the Ghosts of Roman Emperors

Roman emperors' family tree

AUGUSTUS
1ST EMPEROR FROM 27 BC TO 14 AD

TIBERIUS (SON OF LIVIA & STEPSON OF AUGUSTUS)
2ND EMPEROR FROM 14 TO 37 AD

CALIGULA (NEPHEW OF TIBERIUS)
3RD EMPEROR FROM 37 TO 41 AD

CLAUDIUS (UNCLE OF CALIGULA)
4TH EMPEROR FROM 41 TO 54 AD

NERO (SON OF AGRIPPINA AND STEPSON OF CLAUDIUS)
5TH EMPEROR FROM 54 TO 68 AD

Interviews with the Ghosts of Roman Emperors

LIVIA
(3RD WIFE OF AUGUSTUS)

AGRIPPINA
THE YOUNGER
(4TH WIFE OF CLAUDIUS)

Timeline

44 BC
Julius Caesar is assassinated on the Ides of March by Marcus Brutus and others. They hope to bring back the republic, but civil war breaks out.

27 BC
The Roman Empire begins as Caesar Augustus becomes the first Roman Emperor.

14 AD
Death of Emperor Augustus. Tiberius becomes the second emperor.

Interviews with the Ghosts of Roman Emperors

32–36 AD
Estimated date of the crucifixion of Jesus Christ in the Roman province of Jerusalem. The spread of Christianity begins.

37 AD
Death of Tiberius on the island of Capri. Caligula becomes the third emperor.

40 AD
Caligula marches to the English Channel to invade Britain. Instead, the legions collect seashells and he returns to Rome to celebrate a great success!

41 AD
Caligula is assassinated by the Praetorian Guard. Claudius is found hiding in the curtains of the palace and is hailed the fourth emperor.

43 AD
Emperor Claudius orders the invasion of Britain. An army of four legions and approximately 20,000 auxiliaries, commanded by senator Aulus Plautius, lands in Kent. The Romans defeat a large army of Britons in fierce battles.

54 AD
Death of Claudius – poisoned by his wife Agrippina. Her son Nero becomes the fifth emperor.

59 AD
Agrippina is killed by order from Emperor Nero.

61 AD
Boudicca leads a rebellion of the Iceni tribe against the Romans in eastern Britain. After burning down Colchester, London and St Albans, Boudicca is defeated at the Battle of Watling Street.

64 AD
Much of Rome burns. A legend tells that Emperor Nero watches the city burn while he plays a lyre.

Interviews with the Ghosts of Roman Emperors

65 AD
Nero cruelly persecutes Christians and kills his wife, Poppaea, whom he kicks to death after an argument.

67 AD
Nero enters the Olympic games and is named the winner of every event he enters.

68 AD
Widespread revolt forces Nero to commit suicide, ending the Julio-Claudian Caesar Dynasty and sparking civil war.

69 AD
Unrest in Rome sparks mutiny of the Roman army in Britain. Four Roman emperors follow in rapid succession: Galba, Otho, Vitellius and Vespasian. Vespasian, who had led a legion during the conquest of Britain, emerges as the successful leader and begins the Flavian dynasty.

Did you know...
There were about 70 Roman emperors until the last (Romulus Augustus – 476 AD). Septimius Severus was an African Roman Emperor from 193 to 211 AD. He ruled large parts of Europe, the Middle East and Africa. When he came to Hadrian's Wall in 208 AD, there were African soldiers already stationed there, as Roman Britain contained people from various races, including from Northern Africa.

Quiz – Decies centena millia, qui vult vincere?
(Who wants to win a million?)
WHO WANTS TO BE A LEGIONNAIRE?

A legionnaire was a member of a Roman legion, an army of about 5000 professional marching soldiers. Each legionnaire earned around 225 silver denarii a year. No doubt a salt ration was given to soldiers, too – valuable stuff, but as for being paid with lumps of it instead of cash, take that with a pinch of salt!

(You can play this quiz on your own or with a contestant, a question-host and an audience)

Interviews with the Ghosts of Roman Emperors

1. For 100 denarii – Where are many of the first Roman emperors buried?
a) Colchester Castle
b) Behind Luigi's Italian Restaurant in Paris
c) The Arena of Verona
d) The Mausoleum of Augustus in Rome

2. For 200 denarii – How did the Roman dictator Julius Caesar die?
a) Falling off a chariot
b) Eating poisoned figs
c) Being stabbed 23 times
d) Sitting on a snake in the bath

3. For 300 denarii – Who took over as leader in Rome after Julius Caesar ?
a) Queen Cleopatra
b) Octavian
c) Boudicca
d) King Tarquin

4. For 500 denarii – Which of these was a Roman invention?
a) The daily news bulletin
b) Poisoning
c) Spaghetti Bolognese
d) Urine

5. For 1000 denarii – Who was the first Roman Emperor in 27 BC?
a) Julius Caesar
b) Augustus Caesar
c) Septimus Caesar
d) Octopus Caesar

LIVE FROM THE CRYPT

6. For 2000 denarii – Who was the second emperor – named after a river?
a) Thamesius
b) Mississippius
c) Tiberius
d) Nilus

7. For 4000 denarii – Empress Livia died in 29 AD. How is that date written in Roman numerals?
a) XIX
b) XXVIIII
c) XXIX
d) IXXX

8. For 8000 denarii – Emperor Gaius Caesar Germanicus was given the nickname 'Caligula'. What did that mean?
a) Terrible Temper
b) Little Booties
c) Hairy Legs
d) Cute Earlobes

9. For 16,000 denarii – At the age of 28 years, Caligula died. How did it happen?
a) He killed himself
b) His sister poisoned him
c) His uncle threw him off a cliff
d) The Praetorian Guard stabbed him to death

10. For 32,000 denarii – Which of these events was Emperor Claudius NOT responsible for?
a) Throwing Christians to the lions
b) Invading Britain
c) Having his third wife killed
d) Celebrating the 800th anniversary of Rome

Interviews with the Ghosts of Roman Emperors

11. For 64,000 denarii – Emperor Claudius married his niece, who was his fourth wife. Who was she?
    a) Livia Drusilla
    b) Julia the Elder
    c) Agrippina the Younger
    d) Claudia Octavia the Middle-aged

12. For 125,000 denarii – During the reign of Emperor Nero, Boudicca fought his Roman soldiers in Britain. Who was she?
    a) Queen of the Iceni people
    b) Queen of the Ikea tribe
    c) Queen of the Druids
    d) Queen of East Anglia

13. For 250,000 denarii – Emperor Nero tried to kill his mother several times. Which of these methods did he NOT attempt?
    a) Putting a scorpion in her bed
    b) Poisoning her food
    c) Sinking a boat she was sailing in
    d) Making her bedroom ceiling fall on her

14. For 500,000 denarii – Emperor Nero was responsible for killing many people. Which of these did he NOT have killed?
    a) Christians
    b) His wives
    c) His younger step-brother
    d) His father

15. For 1 million denarii – In which year was one emperor murdered, a new emperor crowned and a future emperor born?
    a) 27 BC
    b) 27 AD
    c) 37 AD
    d) 54 AD

Answers:
1 (D) 2 (C) 3 (B) 4 (A) 5 (B)
6 (C) 7 (C) 8 (B) 9 (D) 10 (A) 11 (C)
12 (A) 13 (A) 14 (D) 15 (B)

Oops – sorry, there's no prize money after all as denarii coins were phased out during the Roman Empire's decline. Help yourself to a pinch of salt instead!

Interviews with the Ghosts of Roman Emperors

Glossary

Assassinate
To murder a leader in a secret attack.

Dynasty
A succession of rulers from the same family.

Empire
A group of nations over a large area ruled by one leader or government.

Gallstone
A small stone-like blockage that forms inside the body in the gallbladder.

Gladiator
A Roman who trained to fight, often to the death, to entertain an audience.

Mausoleum
A large elaborate tomb or the building that houses it.

Mosaic
A picture or pattern made from many small pieces of tile, glass or stone.

Republic
A nation in which the leaders who make the laws and run the government are elected by the people.

Senate
A council with the power to make laws.

Toga
A long, loose outer garment worn by citizens of ancient Rome.

In the classroom

10 titles in chronological order:

Tutankhamun
Ancient Egypt and Howard Carter's 1922 discoveries.

Qin Shi Huang
Ancient China and the Terracotta Army discovery of 1974.

Roman Emperors
Ancient Rome and the first 5 notorious emperors after Julius Caesar.

Henry VIII
Tudor England and the turbulent trials of king and country.

Pirates
17th & 18th century swashbuckling on the high seas and the Caribbean.

Queen Victoria
The life and times of an enigmatic queen and her Victorian world.

Louis Pasteur
The age of scientific discovery: disease, germ theory and hygiene.

Sparky Inventors
The age of electricity pioneers; from Thomas Edison to Nikola Tesla.

Titanic
The famous tragedy told by those who were there.

Women Doctors and Medical pioneers
Marie Curie and the first women Nobel prize-winners.

(Arranging the books in order could be an activity in itself!)

Each of these books is primarily for solitary reading, but they have also been designed with the option for groups to read and perform together as a play at school, home or anywhere else.

A whole class can be included, or smaller groups if individuals take on several parts. There are plenty of flexible possibilities to involve as many or as few as required.

The books can be broken up into their various scenes for reading, performing or recording on video or audio equipment separately, simultaneously or with everyone together. On the other hand, one solitary individual could, with different voices, record scenes alone. The ultimate aim is that all who read or perform should be entertained, informed, engaged and encouraged to enjoy plenty of imaginative factual fun.

Ideas for performance

As well as the 20 or so character parts in each book, there is plenty of scope for extra roles for both performers and creators behind the scenes.

Potential extra roles

FACT-CHECKER(S)
Throughout the script, various bizarre facts with unusual information appear. Occasionally a flag/banner could pop up saying 'That's TRUE!' (Maybe with an added comment such as 'Yes, they really did eat x'.) Someone could verify such facts or add an extra detail, then be responsible for holding up the sign at the appropriate time in the show.

CONTESTANTS
A few willing volunteers to sit the final quiz could swot up on information before sitting in the hotseat. If a contestant chooses the wrong answer, a replacement volunteer can take over from where they left off. Four lifelines are available: 50-50 (2 wrong answers removed), ask the host, ask the audience and ask a friend.

Director

A suitable person will need to take control of fitting everything together, making decisions and directing the cast (as well as taking the blame!)

Sound Effects

Someone could be responsible for recording/playing appropriate sound effects, TV jingles and songs/music between scenes or to link sections. Anyone so inspired and skilled could adapt the comic strip sequences for PowerPoint (or some such) visual presentation for showing on screen.

Quiz Host

The questioner can read out each question followed by the four possible answers, or a PowerPoint slide can be prepared for showing each question. A second slide can also be prepared with two wrong answers omitted, should the contestant ask for the 50-50 option. The questioner shouldn't see the answer until the contestant says 'final answer', particularly if the 'ask the host' lifeline has been chosen. If the 'ask the audience' lifeline is chosen, the host asks everyone to vote for each answer in turn by raising a hand (voting only once!). After counting the votes for each question, the host repeats the figures to the contestant. If the 'ask a friend' lifeline is used, the contestant will already have chosen someone in the audience to ask. The host invites the friend to give an answer, checks if they are correct and announces the result.

Additional activities

Character Cards

All the characters in the book (whether a genuine historical character or from the TV team) can be summarised on a card with simple headings, scores and personality characteristics. These can then be discussed, displayed or even 'played' if players compare their cards or devise 'Top Trump'-style activities. Lists of character traits/adjectives can be added, with students having to justify why they have chosen their descriptions. Some examples follow:

CHARACTER CARD	
NAME:	
DATES:	COUNTRY:
STRENGTH	
WEAKNESS	
SKILL	
BIG MOMENT	
QUOTE	

Calm	Silly	Grumpy	Angry
Challenging	Cheerful	Pompous	Clumsy
Confident	Miserable	Tense	Dull
Good-Natured	Capable	Nervous	Lazy
Wise	Charming	Selfish	Shy
Dreamy	Enthusiastic	Caring	Scary
Stubborn	Kind	Clever	Lively
Anxious	Witty	Friendly	Patient
Cruel	Intense	Sensitive	Sleepy
Gloomy	Tough	Argumentative	Giggly
Moody	Domineering	Sarcastic	Bored

Timeline Teaser

This could be a puzzle for individuals/pairs or a timed group competition. It would feature the timeline at the back of the book. A photocopy with a few blanks, together with a choice of answers displayed elsewhere, should keep everyone happily amused, engaged and even enraged! This offers a great way of consolidating understanding of the context of the events in the book.

Match the Meaning

Chopping up a copy of the glossary provides a fun way for students to match words with their definitions, helping to learn key vocabulary and ideas.

Commercial Break

How about developing the advertisements from the commercial break with extra jingles, cheesy ad-talk, dialogue, sketches, slogans and even a few puppets thrown in the mix?

Index

A
Antony, Mark 30–31
Augustus, Emperor 4, 7, 12, 14–16, 21–27, 31, 33, 36–38, 40, 55, 57, 60–65, 67–68, 70, 76–78, 86, 92–98, 113–116, 118, 129, 151–155, 158–160

B
Britain 60, 71, 96–97, 99, 102, 104–106, 108, 161–163
Brutus, Marcus 39, 160

C
Caesar, Julius 15, 29–30, 37–38, 40–41, 47, 51, 62–63, 76, 96, 156, 160, 165
Caligula, Emperor 4, 68–70, 82–89, 101, 114–123, 130, 151, 158 161
Claudius, Emperor 4, 68, 71, 97, 99–103, 105–106, 108, 116, 123–125, 133, 135, 137, 140, 142, 155, 158–159, 161

G
garum 50, 135
gladiators 13, 47–48, 102, 128, 136

N
Nero, Emperor 4, 68, 71, 84–85, 98, 123, 125, 133–134, 137–145, 150–151, 153, 158, 161–163

S
Senate, Roman 38, 78, 120, 145

T
Tiberius, Emperor 4, 16, 65, 68, 73–79, 82–84, 87, 92, 98, 100, 114–115, 122, 129–133, 140, 151–152, 158, 160–161,